Cue Lazarus

CAMINO DEL SOL

A Latina and Latino Literary Series

Cue Lazarus

CARL MARCUM

The University of Arizona Press

Tucson

The University of Arizona Press
© 2001 Carl Marcum
First Printing

This book is printed on acid-free, archival-quality paper.
Manufactured in the United States of America

06   05   04   03   02   01   6   5   4   3   2   1

Library of Congress Cataloging-in-Publication Data
Marcum, Carl.
Cue Lazarus / Carl Marcum.
    p. cm. — (Camino del sol)
ISBN 0-8165-2074-7 (alk. paper)
1. Mexican Americans—Poetry. 2. Young men—Poetry.
I. Title. II. Series.
PS3563.A63665 C84 2001
811'.6—dc21   00-009967

British Library Cataloguing-in-Publication Data
A catalogue record for this book is available from the British Library.

Publication of this book is made possible in part by the proceeds of a
permanent endowment created with the assistance of a Challenge Grant
from the National Endowment for the Humanities, a federal agency.

Contents

II

I

Cue Lazarus

Start this with the invocation:
        a seventy-seven Pinto,
        an eastbound freeway, two boys
a few months from their driver's license.

It happens again because you've
        said it. You sit in the back seat,
        a ghost of red vinyl, to listen
to these boys—one of whom was you,

the one along for the ride—talk
        brave about cheerleaders
        and socket wrenches as they pass
a stolen cigarette between them.

They don't know you're there,
        wouldn't believe in you should
        they look backstage, backseat.
The boys are driving back from an October

orchard where they'd gone to see leaves
        change. You remember: *orange, brown,*
        as though you'd just seen those leaves,
because in this proximity

to yourself—the boy in the passenger
        seat—you are thinking the
        same thing, and each of your in-
carnations feels like they've thought this

before. Your ghost, your present tense
        thinks that maybe this isn't right.
        Now you're along for the ride.
These boys haven't cuffed up against

their own mortality yet, though one
        of them is sick. The other one,
        driving and picking at the thin
hair falling from his scalp, will die

soon, because what lurks in his dark
        blood can be cured by medical
        science. And that cure is what will
kill him, as it leaves him weak,

unable to fight off infection
        in his lungs. But that comes later.
        You are here with them now to find
out what you owe to whom—your life,

mortgaged to one of these boys
        and you've never been able to
        rectify that debt. You are the
stage direction, a ghost backstage,

wanting a spotlight, a soapbox
        a soliloquy. Dissolve
        back into your life, like sugar
in tea—exit this scene now, stage left.

                •

You are the apparition again
        in your mother's house. You follow
        yourself down the yellow hallway
to the ringing phone in the kitchen.

You already know who's calling,
        the way you knew then—when you were
        the self you're haunting. Your friend
is dead. You know this even before

his sister tells you—but because your
        ghost is too close, the boy can feel
        your grief, but can't feel his own.
And you did know then, didn't you?

You knew that morning, that the earth
        awakes closest to the sun—four
        days into every new year.
And Lazarus, dead now, four days.

Roll away the stone. Believe
        in something besides the past.
        Awaken from this dream like
a man called out from a cave.

It happens this way each time:
        a bourbon breakdown in January
        rain—weeping an invocation,
cursing corollary.

•

Can you go to Tom's grave today
        and mandate him back to this life?
        Should you cue him from the wing
like a stage direction? Would he

damn you—a sadness, a gravestone
        on your chest, for calling him
        into this mortal suffering?
If you had been in Houston that day

he'd have died anyway. You're a fool
        to think you can bargain across the river.
        Haunting the past won't stop
it from happening each time, exactly

the same way. Won't stop your heart
       from breaking like a glass decanter,
       brown whisky sliding
mercury across the tile.

Huachuca Blackout

We were heavy then—great heaps of earth
brought forth from a mine—thick and amalgamated.
Stumbling boys in the dark, thinking: *out, me, mine,*
this whole bland town can't taste me anymore.
And we drove away whole weekends.
Down dark highways, cul-de-sacs.
Past markers, reflective signs, warnings:

> *Yield*
> *Do Not Enter*
> *Abandon All Hope*
> *Watch for Falling Boys*
> *Next Services—300 miles*
> *Stop. Men under Construction.*

Bobby took an aluminum bat to the back of the skull.
Remembers his eye hanging down past his cheek.
Left eye. Optic nerve. Dangling—delirious
as white lilies—fingertips slipping orbicular.
He could see himself screaming from eye level.
Then the ringing in his ears. Then nothing.

October smoked a long cigar and I drove
three paranoid miles. Bobby held his eye,
whimpering shotgun. The emergency room
staff laughed like tin trays. I vomited beer
on blue carpet. Culpability leaving me like ether.
I'd have traded every peso of wisdom pilfered
from books and consejos for a cigarette.

                    •

The perspective
Bobby had that drunk-rain night
was something we weren't ready for:

our scared selves grasping for light.
And wisdom, what of it?
We couldn't heed road signs,
much less ourselves. The world
was a symbol we couldn't decode.
There is a music that means this:
dissonant and starless night in the desert.

Roads took us the anywhere else we needed,
shoulder and line, quick and defined.
Highways made sense—composed it commonly—
across black-tar skin. Well past midnight,
State Route 83 beckoned like a quest,
like a siren. There is no other way
we could hear it. Bobby drove
the beat-up sedan, his eye three-weeks
bloodshot. Three hours flat-out of town.
Bridges burning behind us, cigarettes
held out car windows: monolith shadows scurrying
past the bright edges of safety glass.
The heavens inked out.

•

In Hubble's deep field image
there is a galaxy so far away, to see it
takes a theoretical miracle of physics.
The white splinter warps all matter and movement,
fleeing a million light years a second.
And if we could have left town that fast,
if we could have outrun a rum-runner dawn
we'd have understood something
about the lights being out.
Instead, the mountains just seemed big.
And it's enough to feel that small next to rock.
But to feel so small next to light—
we couldn't stand still long enough to see clearly.

Light Show

Sometimes I think of that brick house on the busy road,
where traffic was a constant funeral procession.
The room I rented there—the beat-up
springs of the used-up mattress, that half-covered
the dark stain (we never could identify), on the carpet
where she thought twice about treading barefoot.

I think of how there, in that bed with her
at night, we would watch the bluish slants
—the passing headlights—cast photo-positives
through the venetian blinds: across our bodies,
the mattress, the dirty carpet and up the bare walls . . .

until the ebb and flow of asphalt faded in distance,
                          and the room grew dim and quiet.

Then, we would coo like kittens, pausing only
to let the lights play over us, merely for the pleasure
of not feeling their touch.

Fait Accompli

I could have spread white-sweet frosting over everything.
Grown accustomed to the dusting of flour in the early minutes
of morning. I could have baked my own reasons.

I could have learned to build houses
without nails. Made my passion
for precision fit more than diction.

I could have understudied the bus driver.
learned to lean hard on steel haunches—
holding up traffic, moving the masses.

I could have learned the nuance of bent silverware,
tied off with all night chemists, a match struck
under a spoon. I might have deferred these visions.

I could have specialized myself to Neurology or Cardiology.
Used EKGs and EEGs and MRIs to diagnose myself as mortal.
I could have prescribed my own treatment.

I could have learned to take the snap; to drop in the pocket,
read men's hearts like a defense—step up under pressure,
spiral leather into drama.

I could have called the sky by name. Learned to love equations
because they look like truth. Gathered data on nebulae
and black holes to prove the ambivalence of inner space.

I could have apprenticed myself to anything
and not escaped *the horror and the boredom and the glory.*

Copalquin

December-rain night, I'm driving to the Southside
in search of a cure from my youth. Once, my cryptic abuela
brewed me a remedy for the world—thick and bitter copalquin,
tawny, stringy, bitter root-tea shining in a mason jar—an antidote
for the twist in my spine, the ache in my legs.

What I find is what can't be fixed: the run-down supermercado
on 36th street. Fluorescent lights have buzzed there so long,
they've bleached the air. Yellowed cereal boxes run
down in degrees of Cheerio-entropy. Tomatoes, blanched
by constant noise and light, refuse to ripen. Sallow cajeras
scan UPC after PLU after price-per-pound. The whole store
turning to dingy rice.

Pacing empty aisles, I almost don't notice the late night
exhibitionist. Her mini-skirt, no-panties prancing and her
chulo boyfriend with the Polaroid. I mistake a widower
for Octavio Paz in a security guard uniform—his cart
sparsely filled with cebolla, ajo and cilantro, something
to make the beans taste. And he's holding canned beans,
missing the way his wife would make them con manteca.

In the express lane of 12 dilemmas or less, the *Cosmopolitan*
magazine glosses slick: all cover model and *secrets of asking*
for a raise. The young mother can't take her eyes from it.
Her baby slumped asleep in the shopping cart seat. She mouths
thin wishes, reaches for the magazine and decides against
the frozen potpies, balances the bouncing checkbook in her head
and re-racks the magazine with a sigh—her resignation, bottomless

as my cheap coffee. Her whole life repeats itself like cable programming—
the re-run cadence—in case she missed a package of diapers
or processed lunch meat. They turn up again in her story line,
in the pudding-grubby faces, or the Bud-breath groan

and stubble of her husband snoring while the baby
cries. And she fails the *Cosmo* intimacy quiz.

I'm just the idiot in line behind her, projecting my grocerías
all over this grocery store—as if my sudden repentance
for the new boots and car, the installation of digital-dish
television (there wasn't enough of *nothing* on for me),
could be enough to halt the slow, audible ache in this place.
Only the bagboy and his caterpillar moustache stand out, as he snaps
paper bags to attention, shuffling groceries into dim organization.
The artificial light and sweetener of this animation
hasn't undistinguished him yet. And he thumbs his glasses back up his
    oily nose.

I've found the copalquin—my panacea—but lose something in the drive
    home,
in transition, translation—lost in my Anglicized, agnostic recipe, brewed
    in the
wrong kind of teapot. I'm left to scribble *Pendejo Gringo*—obscene and
    backwards
on rain-fogged windows, rubbing my back against the faithless,
    indifferent dark.

Untitled à la Mode

I say, "We should go for coffee and pie,"
though I know you don't drink coffee.
"Okay, Agent Cooper," you say, and look
at me the way you look at people
on the street—the ones who didn't look
in the mirror before leaving the house.
And this is why I love you.

You entertain my half-baked fancies
like a great-aunt at Christmas dinner,
drunk on eggnog and Kahlúa—you entertain.
So, tonight is à la mode (though you'll order
fries and a diet Coke).

I remember walking the subdivided side streets
of Pacific Beach. The block of poured concrete
stamped W.P.A. 1932. I said, "This is real,
this is concrete imagery." You held my hand
all the way home, while I sucked on the splinters
of an orange-stained Popsicle stick and abstracted
every moment since then.

And now, now you know (though I suspect
you always have), that afternoon the cracked
sidewalk was our little path through the garden.
And tonight, when I ask what kind of pie I should have,
you say, "Apple."

A Prayer for My Brother

When my brother becomes a man, let him find something small,
maybe metal—a wristwatch or swizzle stick—in a shoebox
he's forgotten about. And this small monument he once held
onto, and has perhaps considered tossing out at the end of each
lease, will whisper to him of wind and martinis and the city.
Will whisper to him like the lips of a man he once kissed. And let
him remember how once he couldn't live without this small token
—grant him the memory of signing the credit receipt or slinking
the swizzle stick up a sleeve in a crowded bar. How he smiled
with the weight of possession, a small want satisfied. And let him
smile again as he holds this cold memory, allow him to set the dead
red face of the wristwatch to 3 a.m., or slide the swizzle stick
across his tongue and taste the metallic gin, the lovely sour-salt
olive as it broke, ripe between his back teeth. Confer on him
the moment he was convinced he would always remember, how
he said it out loud, twinkling and drunk. Let this all come back
to him like a dream-song half heard in a winter's sleep.

Magic 8-Balls

That was the summer we shook stick
with James Brown in the slant-eyed sun.
The taste of the break, our congregation—
waiting through the heat for—is this dusk
or twilight? Someone said there was
a difference, subtle as the English on a cue ball
that takes two rails to leave on the eight.

And we shot at 8-balls that had no answers:
mute and dense, mimicked infinity. Is this dusk
or twilight? *Not now James, we're busy. . .*
It's dusk, and we should have been the hell
out of here by now. There's a price on all our heads,
weighing like a pint glass sweating circles on a table.
Twilight time. Who's got next?

The crack of the rack and the scatter. *Get down,
get on up.* This was all Rob's idea—the amber ale,
the cues, the way those balls would throw oblong
shadows over the too much green-between—otherworldly.
"Who the hell do you think you are?" Rob would laugh
after me. Just smile and amble around the table
for the answer. Rob likes to shoot pool because it's

like his painting—depth and structure bleed into form
—an architecture of color and line. He shoots pool to forget
he has to leave his own house every day by five. The live-in
girlfriend needs time to decompress her eight hours, and Rob
feels like he's in the way, or at least his feelings are.
And Tommy's been with a girl now three months,
but hasn't quite figured out how to take her to bed.

The same way he can't figure the bank off
the long rail, and winds up forfeiting in a scratch.

And what is there to say in my defense? Why am I here?
Because I'm the fatalist, and couldn't resist
the cue—weighted and steady, couldn't resist
the idea of amber ale and conversation. Shooting
pool is just a way to ask—
it's in the English, the infamous twilight.

A Prayer for My Laundry

Stain removal is akin to confession.
Begin by remembering each messy transgression
on textile: here, the spot of chili
from the hasty cart—how, for a minute,
you understood clearly cause and effect:
the gravity of beans, the velocity
of a hurried lunch; thick broth
fell and spotted your favorite trousers
—that khaki tweed that's seemed
cursed since purchase: the ghost
of a coffee Rorschach along one thigh,
a mestizo tanned face in the tan
fabric desert, the faded hills of a border birth.

The mind will wander through the laundromat,
an orphaned sock, the clotted blue-gray
lint trap. And here, the dirty collar
from a dirty Tuesday: stress, unstress,
errand and bed. A bit of bleach is needed
to forget the traffic and your own chafed neck.
The brown bourbon and ash from Friday
night's cuff—a bump in a crowd, a splatter
and sway in this winter of auld lang syne.
Here, the yellowed storm clouds basketball leaves
in the pits of white T-shirts; vinegar's best
for getting out sweat.

                    Be grateful now
for each clean shirt—a penance paid
and prayed in a greedy closet, the forlorn
hangers shaking like love letters; feel
the heft of wet jeans, the chemical-fresh
softener, its cruel April scent. And, here,
the warm robe from the dryer—dear and dreaming,

waking late Sunday morning in mismatched
plaids. Take stock of each button and stitch
obligated to pattern. Pray this penance with
folding hands, like a friar sitting stalwart
among the spinning stained glass, the plastic
pews of the bright-quarter laundromat,
patient, and eager for clean habits.

Deliverance and Dr. Porsche

Reverse engineered from the divine: the perfected shut of a Porsche's
    door—
        molding, mechanism, metal.
The sound is gratification. The seat cradles your ass like an end
        to suffering. The click of ignition,
near silent rumble of an engine made to run like God's own wristwatch.
        Feet work through the footfalls
of pedals in the rumba of rpm. Every law of physics induced—
        inertia, speed, time, distance—
on command. All of the pleasure, none of the math. Stomach: delirious,
        mind: drunk on the butterscotch
of leather and coolant. You're pushed back in the seat. It feels as if
        you might die or be born or come.
The night you whispered to the girl with the bourbon eyes.
        And then you die and are born and come . . .
This is Made-in-Germany Zen, a euphoria that fuses you. And you
        bless Dr. Porsche's sweet bald head.

That is what Tom was trying to tell you. But you couldn't translate:
the day he arrived at the door with the 911 he'd borrowed/stolen from
the doctor's house he sat that summer. But you were too practical
or scared and the afternoon newspaper waited in a pile to be delivered.
Tom pleaded with a giddy smile. You just kept folding and wrapping
papers in red rubber bands and this should be a metaphor now.
But it isn't—and the poem fails you, the way you failed to live a little
that afternoon with your friend. The headlines were nothing but tragedy
    anyway,
tragedy that could have waited at least, for a spin around the block.

Remember, this is about getting sideways again in the back seat.
The clammy rush of adrenaline that accompanies out of control.
Deliverance is trust, the conservation of momentum—control
in the swerve—learning how to turn out on the inch of rubber
and asphalt that grip, the thrill of a leather steering wheel regained.

And none of this can save you from the eyes-shut-tight-stop-sign
roulette that makes your chest feel a little hairier. Deliverance
is letting go of the newspaper at the door-stop moment:
a perfect arc, without calculus or a graph—the whisper
across our lips: perfection—what we say when we mean holy.

Interstate Sonnet

A cigarette kiss in the desert. The wind-proof arc
of flame sparks inside the speeding Buick. Menthol:
a break from the monotony of highway nicotine—
most intimate of drugs. Make this mean sorrow
or thermodynamics, whatever small gesture
there is time for. Light another one, the vainglorious

interstate dusk and ash—the long, silver tooth.
This shirtless abandon, this ninety-mile-an-hour
electric laugh. The edges of windshield, haphazard
chatter. The clatter of the hubcap and the thunderclap:
the white-hot retinal memory of your life as a Joshua tree.
Permanence in the passenger seat. This long haul,

this first drag—nothing like cinnamon, nothing
like the iron taste on the back of your mortal tongue.

From: Poetry
To: Entropy

Eventually,
it will all stop,
like the height and class of lighter technology:
the cool, brushed chrome of a Zippo lighter—
still soaked in fluid and wick enough to burn—
but spark engine doesn't respond to thumb,
when the flint runs out, it just stops.

I think this is the way the world will end.

Not only me, the physicists too.
They say energy is never destroyed,
just changed. Changed until it can't be used
by anyone, or anything.

·

That's how we die, just another involuntary action.
And what happens then?
Not just at signs
or the ends of sentences.
It's speculation really, the actuality of it.

That's god, the lack of motion.
Because everything else in the universe moves,
every body, every atom.

I think of the physicist, Enrico Fermi.
He feared the atom would ignite the world.
Though every theory and theology
said it wouldn't.
He feared it though, just for a moment,
and then just for a moment.

Then Enrico was dying.
Dying and reading Tolstoy.
The Death of Ivan Ilych means
that much more when you can feel
your atoms speeding to a stop.

·

Even asleep in your bed you're spinning
at hundreds of miles an hour.
Only your covers and a misplaced faith in gravity
keep you from waking light years
away from yourself.

A dream I had last night:
felt something sharp and cold
in the corner of my eye,
pulled out a five-inch-long silver thorn.

And the dream is stuck in my head.
Like the thorn,
like misplaced faith—
the wondering
what happens when we stop.

For God, Country and Getting Laid

I'm thinking of Pacific islands—the ocean between Japan and Hawaii,
the distance between word and association—like brutality and fragility.
I remember the story my mother told me, about her high school English
    teacher:
how he walked on tip-toe because of World War II.
Captured by the Japanese, the bottoms of his feet, skinned
and convinced at bayonet-point to walk across hot tarmac
seasoned with sea salt.

Follow the map now, to Pearl Harbor, remember? The surprise-debutante
bombing of my state's battleship—now a national memorial
to second opinions. When intelligence is right and ignored,
there will inevitably be memorials. Great granite tombs of memory and
    steel,
the watery grave of desire. And in the skies, that pin-up girl painted on
    the prow
of a fatigue-green bomber—looking back over her shoulder, all cartoon
    curves
and pre-Technicolor lips—glancing back as an invitation

and a warning. The boys on that B-24 had a motto:
"For God, country and getting laid." Every bomb they dropped
was a new pledge of allegiance to that pin-up princess.
To this day, there is a certain length and shade of blonde,
that glimpsed in smoke-dense club-light will turn my stomach callow.
How, like a physicist, we round down the numbers of the heart.
Making each sequential and variable fit neatly into that manipulated
equation we call memory—a distorted color photograph,
candy-coated and redolent. I'm speaking of those celebrated monuments

to mistake, that self-righteous diffusion of fact;
but I forget, we were the country that loaded up
the Enola Gay with fuel and relativity, and introduced
the world to the American version of kamikaze conviction.

Atrocity piled upon atrocity, argument upon argument—
past the point of remedial concrete and flowers.
I remember the blonde bombshell who became my
Day of Infamy, fifty years later and welcomed with open arms.
I think of my country, still making war with history.

We Drove Some Chevys

'72 CHEVELLE MALIBU

Sometimes a Chevy's just a Chevy
one you can take to the river,
and (no surprise) the river is dry,

like the song you just thought of,
it's stuck in your head all the way to St. Mary's
and just past the interstate, the Santa Cruz is dry.

Sometimes a Chevy's not just a Chevy
but instead a '72 Chevelle—eight cylinders,
gray as a ghost, babymoons waxing full

in harsh streetlight. The summer
monsoon tastes green and hot, the desert
in your mouth. A hunch, a thought:
the river is running, brown as a boot.

'64 NOVA CONVERTIBLE

Red, like a marching band, like a bandera,
the kind of red that looks best with green:
it flashed past you down Oracle Road,
stock as the showroom floor, turned
your head like a schoolgirl in a miniskirt.
There are only metaphors to explain
how it was headed south and you were
headed north, the hot wind at your back.
The top down, and driving that machine,
his moustache thin as a wire, sunglasses
on—*perfecto*—was the happiest vato
you've ever seen, the wind in his hair,
the sun entangling the windshield,
exploding the light: a minute-long blind spot.

'74 CAMARO Z-28

Rene bought it brand new. Blue as the ocean
in his dreams. The yellow and white racing
stripe down both sides, fast as a shoplifter.
What better car for the Levy's store detective?

That Camaro ran nearly on machismo
alone, thick as Rene's beard.
How the gringitas loved his dark, good
looks—a Mexican Travolta. My mother's

youngest brother, Rene kept me and my primos
in line without saying a word; he had a stare
that scared you enough to behave, like the stories
I'd hear about my Tata. Once, he caught me
and Johnny in the Camaro's bucket seats,
shifting the tranny, playing with the lights
and *estereo*—what we knew of freedom
was the open road and an open Coors.

"¿Qué están haciendo?" Rene's voice asked
from behind us like a stone. "We were just playing. . ."
Rene looked right through us. My mother said he
smiled only when we walked away.

'67 IMPALA SUPER SPORT

Mayate green, a June bug dance.
That loco worked overtime, worked
double time—we're talking Christmas
and Easter—stocking the aisles

by the pallet-load. Got him a promotion
and a paint-job. Green and gold
like the silken mayates we'd catch
on mesquite bark when the summer

clouds would roil angry in
the Rincons. The three coats of paint
cost a grand apiece, and the wheels?
Olvídate. He got a deal on those.

He went on dayshift and wears
a tie: assistant grocery manager.
He keeps those aisles as straight
as that car. Too bad it's up for sale.

He went and knocked-up his novia,
celebrating the promotion with a case
of Coors and that long back seat.
He keeps telling me about her long

black, black hair and her breath
on his ear, sweet as tequila.
She's a nice girl and all,
pero, man to give up that car?

'69 NOVA

It belonged to my Nino Ramón, originally.
A gift to him from my mother for his departure
to college. She was working then, making good
money counting money for Capin's Department Store.

Ramón installed the dual exhaust
that rattled the windows from the street,
and the sticker in the back window, the fat
circle of an American flag. He grew his hair

long and didn't go to Vietnam. That car,
blue as lightning, crackling across the black
monsoon-summer sky, streaking from Nogales
along the dark summer highway.

Years later, my father took the Nova
back and forth from the air base. The blue
lightning blanched and oxidized by the
jealous summer sun. So my father

stripped the paint down to silvered metal
and primered her white as a sheet—dull
and matte as an old horse, a ghost horse.
I was fifteen, and Tom and I had our eyes

and plans on that car. But the three gears
and eight cylinders were deemed too much
—though I suspect my father
lost the title to a full house against his two-pair.

Mine and Tom's "Deathmobile" never carried
us anywhere, not to the cinema, or stale class-
rooms, or to watch the Pantano fill and run,
flash-flooded—lightning bluing our eyes.

'79 MONTE CARLO

That car was ugly, a big steel
box, but it looked good as a lowrider.
Almost anything looks good
as a lowrider. The Monte Carlo's
one saving grace: the front seats
swivel outward like an office chair.

There's an old joke
that asks why we drive so low to
the ground—it makes it easier
to pick lettuce, *ese.* Why else
would we put a hydraulic suspension
on a car? Go pick your own
fucking lettuce. And we'll pick

up the pretty girls, cruise the boulevard,
and celebrate this life—ripe with summer.

'82 EL CAMINO

It was Tío Cosme's last, quixotic
wish that we load his coffin
in the bed of the El Camino

to drive him to the grave,
draped with the American flag
he'd served all his life.

That El Camino, sliding tan
and immaculate through the streets
of Nogales. Everyone crossed

themselves as Cosme motored by.
Rene, in the driver's seat,
taking his brother for one last ride.

The air, so hot and heavy in May
and the seven guns flaring their three
toned salute, and the flag to my tía,

a dark triangle of midnight.
And I couldn't, for anything,
remember the last time it rained.

Cuando El Presidente visitó a mi pueblo

The day the President came to town, he ate at my mother's favorite
     restaurant.
The local television news was in a frenzy and even the weather
     cooperated.
The President made it a point to come to town for the old people and the
     Mexicans.

It was parade day in town, the rodeo, setting itself off like a wet firework,
but the President didn't come to town to see bucking broncos. His speech
     made him hungry,
and someone told the President to eat at my mother's favorite restaurant.

The old gringos who come down here to retire were worried about their
Social Security, about their Winnebagos and the price of gas. The
     President assured
their gray-haired heads: He'd come to town for the old people and the
     Mexicans.

He looked good, the President, like he'd had some sleep. If I were the
     President
I'd come to Tucson too, in the mood for some good comida mexicana.
The day the President came to town, he ate at my mother's favorite
     restaurant.

They showed the President's lunch ticket on the television news: a taco, a
     tamale,
a tostada, an enchilada, even a chile relleno. And even though I liked the
     President,
it looked like he'd come to town to make a point to the old people and
     the Mexicans.

A taco, a tamale, a tostada, an enchilada, and even a chile relleno. *Mi
     Nidito,* my little nest,

that little cocina down on south Fourth, they were as excited as the rest
    of us that
the President had made it a point to talk to the old people and the
    Mexicans,
that he'd bothered to stop for lunch at my mother's favorite restaurant.

Fellowship

I pass the same black dog
every morning in the uneven
cobbled streets. "Buenos
días," we each seem to say,

I know his bony hips and he
my sleepy smell of cigarettes
and aftershave. We're both
out to scrounge what we can

from the plaza, nosing
into torta carts, then kicked
away with curses. Black dog,
you must have arrived

from across the sea—from that
empirical, salt island—tenant of
superstition. Did it grow tiresome,
being feared by the pious?

At least fear has its modicum
of respect. Here, you've learned
you're just another nuisance
and the table scraps are few

and fought over. I watched you
black dog, out by the basílica,
stumbling upon a cooked chicken
fallen, out of chance or refusal,

into your lucky gutter.
How you looked around
in canine disbelief before packing
off with the pollo hanging slack

between your jaws. You lounged
under the relief of St. Mark
tearing meat, breaking bone,
uncontested.

A Leaving July

A dragonfly twitches umber
in the oleander. Dead blossoms
cast a burgundy litter—a wind-strewn
pattern—soft and humid as yesterday's
mail. It takes moisture to decompose.

Kate decided to get north this summer,
back to Pennsylvania—the state
of getting in the way. In America,
we're guaranteed the freedom to pull up
stakes and leave when the weather gets too hot.

That's how we've translated the pursuit of
happiness. Funny, how we chase after
ourselves like pearlescent marbles round
a dirt circle, someone's rock always
pushing our boundaries. The katydids all

a-jitter, screeing like the city's busted
air-conditioners—the decibel mating dance.
Mesquites, thick with molted shells, already
crumbling. The dragonfly bides its time
for the feast. Thunderheads stumble into

the city, tear their bellies, spill
monsoon into shaded puddles,
into burgundy decomposition—
the katydids sound their dull, hot note.
And the dragonflies, patient as eggs.

A Prayer for my Breakfast

I forget the patron saint of eggs.
Maybe Saint Francis the sissy—
his burlap robes and preemptive
hair-do, the sandals and rope
belt cinched in a knot of faith.
A rope to hang himself with
should the chattering birds and
God's onerous voice get too loud,
should prescriptive poverty become
too much. I'd like to renounce
the salt and pepper shakers
of this life. But the eggs are here
twelve lines into this poem
and getting cold. I love eggs
for their frailty, their used-up
symbolism—over easy, yellow
yolk running like a cold in summer.
This is where I think about the whole
chicken and egg dilemma. Now
they say it was the dinosaurs that
came first—neither chicken nor egg.
This is where someone remarks
on post-modernism. The taped
recording of a record skipping. This
is where someone should laugh.
So laugh. That's self-reflexivity.
This is where I gobble down
the eggs like some clever ferret
who's mastered the cast-iron
skillet and heavy enjambment.
This is where I take my vow
of intellectual poverty, put down
the pen and cross myself out of habit.

II

Dreaming Pancho Villa

The silence that was neither Spanish
nor English
was my prayer.
                    —Luis Alberto Urrea

1.
Last night I dreamt I was Pancho Villa—
ragged, bandoliered, reckless.
I dreamt my poetry at the end of a pistol,
felt it kick nearly out of my hand.

But this morning I awoke again
white and assimilated into these cobwebs
of my half-self. When did I forget
my mother? Sometimes Spanish

syllables creak like wobbly shopping cart
wheels, I have to lean against accent,
fill myself with verbs: *necesitar, hablar, poder.*

2.
Half, *medio,* milkweed,
Carlos Gringo, Carlos Murphy.
Part *mexicano,*
part Kentucky hillbilly,
I've angloed my way
through this life—
hablando español
de conveniencia,
nunca pensando en
la bendición.

3.
I dreamed again last night
I was Pancho Villa. Only this time

I couldn't speak a word of Spanish.
I could understand what the men
were asking me, but to blurt orders
in English would have stretched my neck.
So I kept quiet, austere. I kept a rifle
in my hand. I've taken it as a sign.

When I was fourteen,
I lost my brand-new Timex
in the waist-high surf of Pismo Beach.
I couldn't feel it missing from my wrist
until I was in my uncle's Volvo,
my shorts still soaking, my lips caked white.

The sand in my hair, the sand in my shoes—
the very real estate of Madera, where
during the revolution, no train or telegraph
passed for months. The business
lumbering on, turning trees
to the fabric of living.
After the war, they sent query
to Juárez, they needed the hour, the day,
the month, the year they hadn't noticed.

4.

I'm awake early, half-dreams of last night's rain & a dirty porch pull me
from the sheets. *En la madrugada,* a broom is a necessary instrument.
The swish of straw against concrete, a whisper, a prayer. Shoulders
cantilever, wrists rigid, hands in pliable tension—in this motion there is
memory.

My great-grandmother swept her porch, the way she did every morning.
From the burnished Sonoran dawn, a stranger approached. She watched
him, always sweeping. The man was young, in his early thirties maybe,
beaten, ragged. His face crusted with blood, filthy. The man appealed to
her, *"Señora, por favor, ayúdeme,"* he said. She stopped sweeping &
looked at him. *"Me siguen los federales,"* he said. She looked on him with

pity & brought him into her home. She must have thought of her daughters, she must have thought of consequence. She put the man in a bed, went back outside to sweep. The federales arrived shortly after, five on horseback armed & angry. "*Señora,*" they asked, "have you seen a stranger this morning?" She stopped sweeping, told them she had not. They asked if anyone was in the house. "No one," she told them, "only my sick uncle." They left without incident or investigation.

Night fell. She cleaned the man's wounds, gave him clothes, listened to his stories of revolution. She told him, "Whether the revolution or the government, I lose chickens all the same." She handed him a plate of *arroz con pollo*. He rested for two days. She gave him the few centavos she had & he left amidst the desert night.

Years later, the man returned to her house—with a gift that no one can remember—to thank her for his life.

5.
This time it's turning
tequila *sueño,*
gold spinner
gone retrograde
illusion.
La Sirena—verde-verdad,
glinting back-black
and skin—
across the metallic blue
chulo wagon.
Mariachi gone mad
in the back seat.
This is cruising
at watch-me-
miles-an-hour.

"*Ese,*
why don't
you come down

to chrome avenue,
where it's all
manos y moda?
We'll sit
straight-slick,
three-reefer-
tone-deaf-
brass-stick high.
Me and you, *pendejo.*
We'll pick up Hi-Tone,
all fingers and hair,
that little *guitarrista.*
No te mortifiques,
Ride shotgun with me.
Pégame un grito."

Chale. I've got work to do, homes.

6.

7.
I'm dreamsick now. Staying asleep past
noon. *Desvelado.* Headache-fog
when I'm awake, even keeping down
milk is hard. Images, sounds, curdle thick
in my ears, my eyes. *Levántate.*
¿Qué horas son?

I dream Villa's first murder. The other
man on horseback, his *jefe's* son. An argument
at the crossroads. A girl, Pancho's sister.
Something forced—a point, a pistol. A sharp
report, blue-black smoke. Fear, alarm—the smell

of guilt, like bad *masa,* taints tastes, turns on Pancho.
Running now, like before but worse. Three days
into *las montañas. Marcado por vida.*

8.
In a dream of brown skin, I'm lost
in black, black hair, dark nipples,
a face I've never known. A kiss
so difficult I moan. My face
wet with her—princess, *mujer*—irrecoverable.
Only impression across
sleep-soaked lips, only an ache
and a dark, dark scent.

9.

10.
Barbed wire fence runs down the axis
       of a heart. River rides in canyon
       dreams—a revolution in water.
I am a kiss, confessed by tongues that will not pronounce me.

Last Days of Summer
for Stephanie

We spend the last days of summer
in a room small and square as a cell.
Lovers sentenced to a double bed
and slow ceiling fan. We are absconded.

But from what? The hot doldrums?
Tedious summer television, the whirl
of idleness? Today, it's enough to be
quaint, inspired by the foreign

minutiae. The *No Parking* signs, houses
leaning straight against hillsides,
the lemon in tea and the ice—somehow
more captivating away from home.

Your face, your arched eyebrows
and back against a hotel bed and the
ceiling fan in its slow circles. The wisps
of cigarette smoke trailing like film noir.

As if I'd noticed them for the first time
—or the last. The space between us:
the way our exhalations mingle mid-sentence
in our slow rhythms: a girl pacing

the double-helix of double-dutch jump ropes
for the moment of merging. Now the perspiration
on your upper lip when you come—eyes
shut tight against pleasure, as if to open them

would colorize our sepia-toned existence. We linger,
languid as cats. The red light from the balcony casts
a slow beacon in case this all burns up. A moment
in the dark as you doze against my arm.

And light, like something held close—a pillow,
a peach, wet and warm as a kiss. The light,
a navigation point back to our everyday:
our course written in wrinkled sheets.

Leeward

Wind enough to set sail, but I suppose
I'm not the best judge of passage
toward good intentions. I know about
intention and the sleight of hand required
to dance the cable along my fingertips
as the sail lifts and opens. A line is drawn
between me and the patch of nothing
where I work. And suddenly, I'm aware
of harnessing nothing in my last life.
Now, on a deck that moves without me,
the lighthouse has become its own
                constant reminder.
And isn't that the story of the mind? A light
that oscillates outward, sharp as grief;
a beckoning toward unsteady horizons.
But I aim for them, like Ulysses, with only
a vague sense of direction. I practice
tying myself in knots, a useful skill
for those who have forgotten which way is up.
I hope that what I have come to know
about the sea isn't just metaphor
from Nantucket graveyards, or symbol
taken from the salt-smoothed stones
                at Pismo Beach.
Wasn't it Columbus who proved the world
weary, stale, flat and unprofitable?
Now I've put this mutiny of one to bed.
In the morning, oysters offer themselves, shells
gleaming like rain-slicked nights. Pearls in hand
I'm beginning to understand grace
                and consequence:
the way a dog understands—only after having
his face rubbed in the mess of himself.
Voices rise into matins fog, and every fragment

of truth I grasp is sharp and shiny.
The clatter they make as they fall
seems to herald the arrival of direction—
a compass that reads itself,
a triangulation of the human heart.

Pentecost

It must be messy being an angel,
the tips of your wings
always flecked with blood.

•

I'm seeing them everywhere,
catching them in my peripheral vision—
disheveled, dirty needing a shower
and a place to crash.
But when I turn to focus,
to look at them properly,
they're gone. Gone or never
really there, like a shadow's shadow.

It must be hard being an angel.
They want to be taken seriously,
did you ever think of that?
Taken seriously when they order a burger
or bump into you in a crowd.

Maybe I'm wrong.
Maybe it's us who want—
want to be taken seriously.
Maybe we have to
because the angels won't.

They're tired, you know.
Tired of having salt
slung in their faces.
Tired of watching over
the shoulder of ignorance
and mistake. Tired
of saving us from

the impending trains of our lives.
Tired of us saying, "Thank God."

•

My friend James was minding
his own business
of gray parrots, counting
their syllables and requests,
when he was interrupted
by a slack thud in another room.

Outside the thick, paned glass
an angel lay crook-necked
and soaking in its own primordial fluids.

Jim freaked.

He expected a pigeon
maybe a brown-dusty dove,
but not this.

Filled with the strange guilt
of modern living and years
of corporate Catholicism,
he wrapped the heavenly corpse
in a sheet, wrestled his dead weight
into the desert and dug.

"I buried it," he told me
over two too many drinks.
"I couldn't think of what else to do."
We all have encumbrances we drag
out into the desert: things we don't
understand and don't want to deal with.
Things the authorities can only make

more troublesome. The things that smack
up against the windows of our lives;
not knowing in from out,
their dull thuds demanding attention.

And aren't we like that angel?
Bumping up against change
just hoping it doesn't kill us.
Trusting we'll crash through
to the side of ourselves we can see.
Emerging cut and bleeding,
elated just to be alive.

This is what I mean by *Grace.*

•

Williams once said
that poets see with the eyes
of angels. Now, I'm wondering
if angels are blind.
I wonder about the old man
I run into now and again,
about what's under his reflective vest.
Is he hiding milky orbs
behind his blind-man's glasses.
How blind is justice?
How blind is love?

I met a man who claimed
to have survived intercourse with an angel.
He told me about that woman
and the wings tattooed on her back
from her shoulders to her ass,
he said they were more than blue ink.
They were real, folded, hiding—

he said it was the best sex
he ever had. He told me
his soul still aches.

I don't believe him. I can't.
I'm jealous. Jealous that he
can ache inside, like a stomach,
like a mended bone before the rain.

And for a moment, I can see.
See how an angel might rationalize,
not wanting to realize,
that for an angel, to ache once
is to ache forever.

●

Pride, the sin of poets,
the sin of angels.
What can I say about sin
that hasn't been covered
by theology and poets
more brave than me?
Not much.
I'll say it though.
Say it to hear myself.
Say it because I'm prematurely old.
Say it because I've sinned
like an angel—not once doubted,
not once had my judgment clouded.

Say it because I still do.
Make my sins of passion
and liberty—sin because I can.
Indulge myself in black suits
and sweet bourbon. Smoke

cigarette after cigarette
without ignorance. Slept
'til five in the afternoon
without fatigue.
I've skipped towns and tabs
omitted whole years of my life.
I've sinned until it hurt,
but I've never really ached.

Infocalypse Now

My ideology is a road
fallen into disrepair, uneven and ugly.
The world rushes to meet me
in a Technicolor wave
—the too-warm sun of December,
the mud-splattered sides of my car.
Driving along at 40 miles an hour seems absurd—
the complexity of fuel injection,
the physics equations themselves.
Rocketing past the billboards of reinvention
that promise value meals and good time cigarettes
and shopping malls filled
with what poets need.
I'm painfully aware of being unaware
—shifting gears and changing
lanes, breathing. Suddenly
small and insignificant as the splashdown of Icarus,
puttering through the construction miracle of my apartment complex,
and I wonder if I should have a complex about my apartment.
Struggling up the stairs
like a half-fixed junkie. Meeting visions
of Eliot and Lowell, Neruda and Paz,
all black and white shades of gray
—beggars on the median of Limbo,
holding shabby signs: WILL WORK FOR TRUTH.
And I'm ashamed at having none to give.
Fumbling with my keys at the door
—jingle-jangling,
slick as nightsweats, shivering in the shade
of something as simple as being overwhelmed.
I slip inside, peeling off books and clothes—
naked in fluorescent light,
looking mad and jaundiced.

And I remember how mirrors
and photographs lie. Lie like the life
I've learned to hold in my hands, as real
and phenomenal as chocolate.

Pound, in his eighties, visits Harvard

He is haunted—eyes
the color
of stagecraft
—distant, flat-dark
and dense
as diesel fuel.

He still functions,
still feeds himself,
controls cutlery.
Still puts on
those tweed-
brown pants,
ties his own shoes.

He doesn't talk.

He's run out
of words. Language
left him like a grocer,
twisting in linoleum
light, wondering, *how much,*
how much
for these beans.

He sees angels
squatting in trees,
but has run out
of words,
of faces.

He is a lover,
turned out

by midnight
discord, searching
night-blind
for a pen.

Unrequited Elegy with Gatsby's Shirts

I know how you wanted her. Those billboards of reinvention
that crowd the avenue eyesores—I know you were driving.

Hot August Sundays are interchangeable from the city to East Egg:
the dark ache in an impossible pink suit, pining at a window

from the tree line; the moonlight whispers something altruistic.
I've heard that same whisper crouched low in my teenage Toyota,

parked down the street from a girl's house, watching a single
lighted room in the too-late hours. How it smelled like the oil

ticking in every engine from here to the eastside. The green light at the
      end
of her dock was as close as you dared get—but the self you'd baked

from scratch required validation. Once, in my newest incarnation,
I was a measure away from telling that girl, "I have something to give
      you,

I don't want it anymore." Five years of rehearsal failed me. I balked
in that space between breath and kiss. Because the truth is, I might

as well have thrown a crumbling brick, *love me* scratched across one
face in indelible ink, right through her window. I should have shattered

that winsome torture, with the reality of her lips, the violence of her
freckles against my cheek. But I wouldn't have my threadbare self,

newly elaborated and finally workable, undone by something as difficult
as a kiss—five years in its coming. I should have shattered the space

between us like an accident. I was a measure away, her waist and hips,
the reality of her lips—a tailor ripping the seams in a shirt sleeve.

I might have shattered the space between us, I should have thrown that
    brick.

I know how you wanted her. Your greatest moment: casting those brand-
    new
shirts across the bed—they fell like invention—sleeves, collars and cuffs,

broadcloth and oxford, every color, weave and print. An avalanche of
    cotton
and almost. You hoped she'd pick just one favorite, one you could slip

your arms into with a flourish of stiff starch, because in that color and
    cut
she would love you. Instead she cried at all your beautiful shirts. You
    couldn't

know the space between you was already a boot—stuck in the estuary
    past.
I imagine floating silver and pneumatic, alone across the pool. Watching

the tawny autumn fall consequently across the water; falling stiff and
    regal
as shirts across a bed. We should both be stoned for pride and omission.

Caliginous Sketch

The pencil shavings are piling up around
        the legs of the easel. My friend has been
sketching, manic with each wailing sound
        Miles Davis trumpets out like vehement sin.
Some entity has begun to take shape—
        a face, eyes like dirty glass, a mouth, lips
                a study in mottled ash. More pressure
for the brow, dense and glossy. The nape
        of a neck falls like hair, moves like hips
                under his fingers, under each long measure

of lead that dusts the edge of a hand, a wrist
        bent in classical pose. My friend has never
looked so zealous. Perspiration, a mist
        has beaded against his cheeks, under the clever
dark frames he wears—an affectation.
        He leans back and lights a joint, rolled tight,
                skinny as a tine. He takes the thick
charcoal pastel lightly in contemplation.
        The outline of a breast seems to fight
                against the gravity of his hand, a trick

of light, of buffed shadow. An anatomy
        of desire has emerged across the page,
out of groggy coffee, sips of monotony.
        And in the ashtray the joint burns like sage.
A postmodern Pygmalion, my friend
        considers the woman issued from dust.
                He brushes a hand across her gray form
to blur the lines, to smooth a discriminate end
        to this sketch, this sudden, proximate lust.
                She is the color, the exact shape of a storm.

Marc Antony, Beached

The sky skewed, like a blue veranda. What was anticipated:
his victory, resounding. *There are two ways out of this.*
Now he's pitched upon the beach, deliberates the smack of defeat.
It cuts and festers the corners of his mouth, grits his teeth with
     windburn.
He scratches his neck, chafed armor-sweat and stubble.
All is lost. And ambition—her face—wrenches him. He could
never be full enough, could not resist her lengthy taste.
Whose sword was this anyway? Ambition the lunge,
vanity the parry. And her face, somewhere between:
refined alloy—spine and appetite. *All is lost.* His man wades
to fish. Fish to roast on wet timbers that will not take.
Wet wood is cautious. He was never wise or humble or discreet.
The mackerel stare at him, blank as mica. His own heart: a tinderbox
for her almond eyes and ribald mouth. The tides' rhythms:
the ruinous, the ruinous. And the shipwreck of his life
sullies the sky—skewed blue veranda. *All is lost.*
There are two ways out of this: by sword, and by sword.

Última Llamada
para Lencho Félix

He spends the evening measuring out
jiggers and pints well into the night.
Wiping down the tired mahogany

with a damp, sour rag. Listening
to liars and braggarts, lighting
their cigarettes, then one of his own.

This is how he pays the bills: quarter
by quarter pile up the pickle jar.
Tips, he has lived on tips his entire

life—the cold, silver sentiment
gratitude leaves with its whiskey
breath. When the hour rolls around,

when the last *catrín* takes the last
girl home and the last *borracho*
stumbles down the dark street,

he closes the cantina, runs a hand
through his hair, thinning at the temples—
still immaculate—lights a cigarette, pours

himself a thick rope of whiskey.
It helps the new distress in his chest,
the coughing knot he hasn't told

anyone about yet. Hank Williams
drags out the last sorrowful note
from the scratchy jukebox. He wipes down

the stools, the tables, counts out quarters:
electric bill, new shoes for Ramón,
el mandado. He'll have to cut hair

this month in the shop to get Hellie
her birthday present, then all through
December and January *para pagar las cuentas.*

He coughs so hard he gasps, drinks down the
last burning, brown slug—it loosens
the knot. He stamps out the cigarette.

These damn cigarros me están matando:
he considers the ember, the crumbled ash.
He looks away, outside past the rain,

smiles at the thought of his wife,
how he suddenly misses her
nagging, beautiful face. He hasn't

seen her since morning, when they
shared café con leche and a kiss before
kids rattled out of their rooms. It's late

now, they'll all be in bed. The barber
pole will be turning in the morning,
and he comes in for Joaquín at five

to tend bar. He half-sighs, half-coughs.
Blacks out the lights, turns the key in the lock.
Cold November already. He pulls his coat
collar up to walk the wet night home.

Acts of Contrition, a Beggar & My Brother

A man, his voice dull as concrete, sloughs through beat poetry—badly. & it's because I'm annoyed that I notice the vagrant in the café doorway. He puts two fingers to his mouth, "a cigarette? Just one," he fingers. I don't want this, I don't want to be the one who's noticed. & now, the vagrant in the doorway knows, saw me glance at the open pack on the table. He's an opportunist, a vulture. He descends straight down on me. "Can I have one?" he asks, a six-year-old in need of candy.

*   *   *

Just this afternoon: my brother pulls the smoking hulk of his '65 Plymouth into my life. "My car's freaking me out," he says. & I don't know why he's brought it to me—I don't know the subtleties of a wrench. I guess that the rising, rope-thick plumes are steam instead of smoke & I tell him to come inside & let it cool down. So in the living room my brother flips through channels. While in the kitchen, I'm up to my forearms in hot dishwater. & suddenly, his automotive intrusion isn't about the grease & bone of that Plymouth Fury. I want to tell him I'm sorry. Sorry I was too concerned with my own tie to teach him the elementary half-Windsor. Extend my apologies for being seventeen when he was ten. But somehow I know, however I think I may have failed him, it's my own opinion of accountability I've betrayed. I want this scalding water to absolve me: to make my hands new & pink & pruned—just clean.

I bring out a suit I've outgrown, olive creases still sharp from the dry cleaner. I ask him, "Do you want this, it doesn't fit me anymore." He offers me a cigarette & we light up in front of the bathroom mirror. I teach him that half-Windsor & a four-in-hand. My brother fumbles with the ends of the tie, pulling around and through in a chunky, awkward knot—I wonder why & how I've avoided this—love's small tax of inconvenience.

*   *   *

I give the beggar a cigarette, the way anyone would, just hoping it's enough to make him leave. On his way out, he hovers in the doorway, looks back into the café at the man reading poetry, laughs a fat, dirty-faced laugh. "Hey man, I'm tryin' to read," the man says. "Well fuckin'-a man," the vagrant mumbles & stumbles out into sodium streetlight. I watch him through the open doorway—the flash of a match, the curls & clouds of a first drag. & as he steps into the street without looking, I realize the liability I've accrued.

A Prayer for My Wife

Promise me one thing, that if I should leave
this uncommon life before you, you'll fashion
an old box with the cool, black knit of my
favorite suit, and place inside it my things of this world:
the monogrammed lighter you once gave me
on my birthday when we were young; my wedding
ring; the bronze Washington Monument statuette/thermometer
Tom brought me from his trip; my best-loved
cuff links, the ones that have the face of tiny
typewriters. An empty bottle of bourbon
from the wake, the stale Marlboros
I kept hidden in a desk drawer. The accessories
that made me the small-time Pharaoh in the
khaki desert where we met. I will
always remember you like this: falling
asleep in the old brass bed we inherited
from some great aunt or other, your bare shoulder
peeking from covers, almost coy—the white
Christmas lights I'd strung through the headboard for
that impressionable, Bohemian light,
spread like good candles through the room; the cat,
aloof in the arch of your foot. I'll remember
how my heart swelled (the way poet's hearts
must fight against from time to time
—the sentimental, the precious) how then,
I looked at you and kissed your brow
before I rose from bed to tend this supplication.

Art of Dying

I think of my best friend, when we were sixteen.
Tom drowned in lungs full of his own blood,
sealed off in a plastic box in a Houston hospital.
The day he left, he told me
"I'll see you soon." I always knew when he was lying.
I was a thousand miles away when his mother
tore through that plastic curtain and held her dying son.
A pure, poetic pieta—he didn't die of leukemia.

I also think of my favorite uncle, who outlived
his own father by a year. Tío Cosme died
at fifty-seven, Tata Lencho at fifty-six. An American
dream come true for a Mexican immigrant.
Every generation dying a little better
than the one before. I watched my mother, watching her
father die for the second time. My uncle's black
smoked-out lungs pinned up on a
light station in x-ray splendor. She said
it happened just the same when my Tata died.
I never met my grandfather, except in grainy
black and whites, or in the mirror
at the right time of day. My uncle had a vision;
it wasn't the drugs, it was poetry. He was having
a smoke with my Tata and a cousin named Oscar.
Enjoying the last cigarette, like a poem
no one could write. Don't ask me why I smoke.
I know the poetry won't kill me.

Caw & Crow

I am a crow of a man,
        Hamlet's last, best interpretation.
        Preferring my body
                the color of absence,
dark and disconnected
        as a phone line, as a blank shack.
        Attracted by the sharp, the shiny
                —chrome and chrome's likeness—
the dark reflection of self in small things.
Listen; the finish of this lighter
        doesn't show much else besides
        the truth: it's a luminous machine
        and burns at a simple, exact task.
I've taken to skipping Sunday Mass
and the buckles on my shoes, the straps
remind me of the vows I've vowed against
        —when I write about a man
                smoking a cigarette, I mean
                my grandfather's gray wool suit,
I mean me: too distracted by the glittered cleavage
of stones, by what's been revealed,
        how it's accrued—listen, a crow
will land in December snow to leave
                an angel's print, clear and cold
        as the light between pines.
Throaty calls break the air like flint—strike and spark
—in the cryptic woodcutter's cottage
        grandfather serves his penance,
                splitting wood for fires that will not burn.

Self-Portrait with Lencho and Two Trains

I. Lencho, Abstract

The arms come down
across the tracks,
the air, clanging,
red and cold. Then the train
—each diesel engine
clamoring its one-gear song.
The wheels turn
along their steel grooves
like hands through hair.

The sky falls in fat
drops across the split
Chevy windshield.
The man inside
dials the radio
to pick up a broadcast
from el otro lado,
the post-war static
clings like the soft,
Rubenesque rain
against chilled glass.

It's not raining hard,
not yet. But, the man
can feel the black winter
front coalescing in his
lungs. It's cold there,
he thinks, in his chest
—where he draws
each sharp breath—
like the San Francisco
Bay, when snow falls

over the sea, when the sky
goes the color of slivered shale.

The train is still moving by:
Union Pacific Union Pacific,
painted specific along
each rust-mottled hull.
The rail's slow, clunky rhythms
echo their whispers,
their secrets in the man's ears.
Punctuated by dense, wet
thumps from the clouds, as if
the sky wished to provide
a syntax to the song—the long,
numb cargo confessing
its sins along the tracks.

The man strains to hear
the exclamation the caboose bell
peals. He cracks the acute
vent-window and leans
to listen. Nothing at first,
except the misty
shrapnel rain becomes
as gravity prevails
across the car. Then,
there it is—a broken
schoolhouse counting
to *two,* again and again.

The end is near, he can hear
it ringing. The man coughs
loose, wet and cold. And coughs
again, this time harder.
Harder than the rain.
He catches his breath

long enough to light
a smoke, trailing disparate,
like a specter out the vent-window.
And the caboose goes by,
suspended, blinking its last,
blank, Morse code. *Where,*
the man wonders, *where
will this train stop?*

II. Suburban Station

Wind lashes off the river's
mouth, burning my cheeks.
You walk quickly through
the narrow streets, because,
well, it's cold out. Cold
and Philadelphia dirty.
As if the city built itself
from the gray grief of its
historic, bronze citizens
—posed and frozen.

We duck into Suburban Station.
The concrete stairs are worn
out of the wind. We buy
our automated tickets with
the awkward attention of tourists.
You look flushed and tell
me that even your eyeballs
are cold, in that funny, complaining
voice you get and I laugh.
We sit close together on the bench
in the yellow station. I ask you again
if this is the right stop—just
because I love to hear you
say yes, like New Year's Eve.

The train's light pushes hard
through subway dark, its echoes
piling off the concrete landing.
I watch the light grow louder
and you bend the brim of your
wool hat against the lean of my
shoulder. Here it comes, I say
as if arrival needed a witness.

The cars stop with the pneumatic
complaint of brakes and doors
open with an airy sigh. My attention
is brought over my shoulder,
two days of stubble catch against
the collar of my scratchy coat.
There, against the station's wall,
a man in a gray greatcoat, a fedora
pushed up on his brow like the
impossible angle of a halo.
As his lighter's hood
closes over the flame
with a snap, his dark eyes catch
my gaze. And he waves
as I shuffle onto the train, as if
he knows me and where I am going.

Notes and Translations

Cue Lazarus: The form of this poem is adapted from the envelope quatrains Tennyson used in the poem *In Memoriam.*

Fait Accompli: The last line is a quote from T. S. Eliot.

Interstate Sonnet is an adapted Shakespearian sonnet. Long-distance driving tip: alternating menthol cigarettes with regular cigarettes will keep your mouth from tasting like an ashtray.

Cuando El Presidente visitó a mi pueblo: President Clinton visited my hometown of Tucson, Arizona, in February of 1999, the first visit by a sitting president since Eisenhower, and he did eat at my mother's favorite restaurant.

A Leaving July is for Kate Rosenberg.

Dreaming Pancho Villa: Section 1, *necesitar, hablar, poder*—need, speak, will. Section 2, *hablando español de conveniencia, nunca pensando en la bendición*—speaking Spanish out of convenience, never thinking of its blessing. Section 4, *en la madrugada*—at dawn. Section 5, *La Sirena*—the mermaid from the children's card game Lotería; *verde-verdad*—green-truth; *manos y moda*—hands and style; *no te mortifiques*—don't worry; *pégame un grito*—give me a yell (as in a mariachi yell). Section 7, *desvelado*—sleep-deprived; *levántate*—get up; *marcado por vida*—marked for life. Section 8, *mujer*—woman.

Unrequited Elegy with Gatsby's Shirts is for Marie McMahon.

Infocalypse Now: The title of this poem is taken from the cyberpunk novel *Snow Crash,* by Neal Stephenson. The poem is for Tom Collins.

Last Days of Summer were spent in the Copper Queen Hotel in Bisbee, Arizona.

Leeward is for James Naughton.

Caliginous Sketch is for RKF III.

Marc Antony, Beached: After the Egyptian armada commanded by Marc Antony was defeated by Julius Caesar, Marc Antony voluntarily marooned himself and his valet on a beach some fifty miles outside Alexandria before returning to Cleopatra in her capital city.

Última Llamada—Last Call; *el mandado*—the groceries; *para pagar las cuentas*—to pay the bills; *me están matando*—they are killing me.

Caw & Crow is a fairy tale, and is for Eric Brunet.

Acknowledgments

Many thanks to the journals
and publications in which these
poems or versions of these poems
first appeared:

The Lucid Stone: "Fait Accompli," "Art of Dying"
Shades of December: "Infocalypse Now," "From: Poetry To: Entropy,"
    "Light Show"
Blue Mesa Review: "Dreaming Pancho Villa"

Particular thanks to Gary Soto and the Chicano Chapbook Press
for their publication of a small volume of work, *El Medio Reza*.

A scholarship from the National Hispanic Scholarship Fund
made the writing of these poems possible, as did the
Poetry Center Fellowship from the University of Arizona.

Many people helped make this manuscript possible:
Tom Collins, Maggie Golston, Heather Brossard,
Eric Brunet, Kate Rosenberg, RKF III, D. Shayne Christie, Gabe Neises,
    and James Naughton.

Special thanks to my professors:
Alison Deming for determination
Jane Miller for vision
Steve Orlen for precision
Boyer Rickel for grace
Richard Shelton for generosity

Thanks to my family. They may not always
understand what I do, but they let me do it.
And to my second family, the Foleys—this book
is for our man Thomas.

Finally, to my wife, Stephanie—
you keep me honest, you keep me vital.

About the Author

Carl Marcum was born in Nogales, Arizona, and raised in Tucson. He attended the University of Arizona for both his undergraduate and M.F.A. degrees. He is currently a Wallace Stegner Fellow at Stanford University and lives in a poky little town three exits south of San Francisco.